Just Say No!

Just Say No!

More Cartoons by Pat Oliphant

Andrews and McMeel
A Universal Press Syndicate Company
Kansas City

ISBN: 0-8362-1700-4

Library of Congress Catalog Card Number: 92-72249

ATTENTION: SCHOOLS AND BUSINESSES

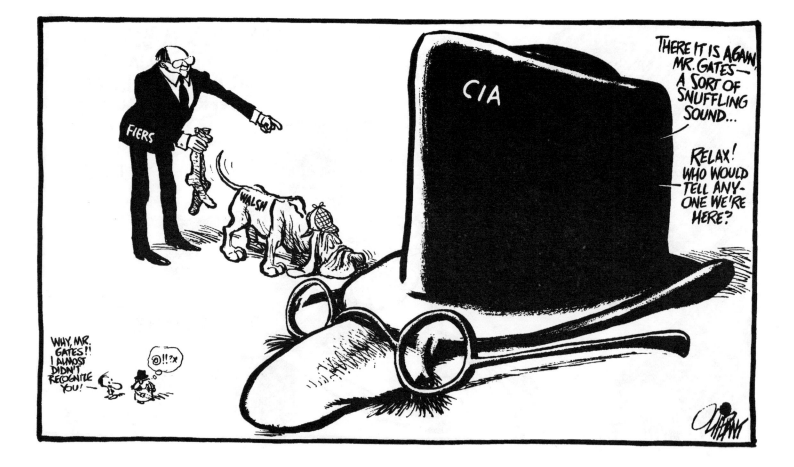

..AND SO THE SENATE, WITH GRITTED TEETH, VOTED ITSELF A $23,200 PAY RAISE.

'BOOTSTRAPS GORBACHEV... WHAT D'YOU THINK?'

July 24, 1991

August 1, 1991

CONSERVATIVES (OURS)

CONSERVATIVES (THEIRS)

START.

14

THE CAT WHO KEPT COMING BACK.

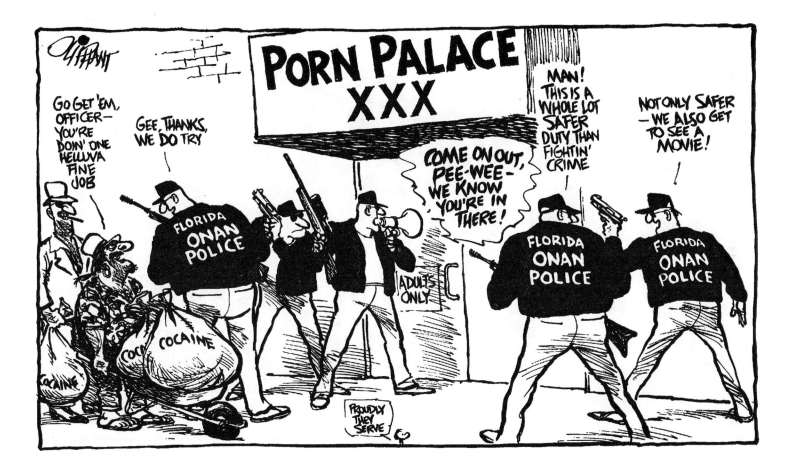

August 14, 1991

18

'LOOKS LIKE THAT MR. QUAYLE WAS RIGHT... WE'RE GONNA HAVE TO SPRAY FOR LAWYERS!'

August 17, 1991

'ANOTHER HUNDRED MILLION BIG MACS, AND GET THE MESSAGE TO CONGRESS
WE CAN'T DO ALL THIS ON OUR OWN!'

'PRIMA BALLERINA GORBACHEV HAS CALLED IN SICK. DANCING IN HIS PLACE THIS EVENING ARE UNDERSTUDIES YANAYEV, KRYUCHKOV, PUGO, PAVLOV, STARODUBTSEV, BAKLANOV...'

NICE SHOT, MOTHER RUSSIA.

WHEN MR. REPLOGLE, THE GLOBE-MAKER, BROUGHT IN THE SEVENTY-THIRD CHANGE OF THAT DAY, MISS MUNCH IN THE PAINTING DEPARTMENT QUITE SUDDENLY LOST IT.

September 2, 1991

'HEY, EVERYONE! REMEMBER HOW WE SAID WE'D LOVE TO GET OUR HANDS ON THOSE NASTY LITTLE COMMIE APPARATCHIK SUPERVISORS FROM THE HEROIC PEOPLES' SHIRT FACTORY...?

'BAD NEWS, O, GREAT ONE — THE DREADED THYROID IS ACTIVE AGAIN!'

September 25, 1991

'MR. SHAMIR WANTS SOMETHING POSITIVE IN THERE ABOUT SETTLEMENTS ON THE WEST BANK!'

September 27, 1991

October 3, 1991

'GOOD LUCK, SIR.'

THE CONGRESSIONAL DINING SCENE.

October 10, 1991

'DAMMIT, SENATOR— I BELIEVE WE'RE IN ANOTHER OF THOSE CYCLES!'

October 14, 1991

'...OR WE COULD QUIT WHILE WE'RE AHEAD.'

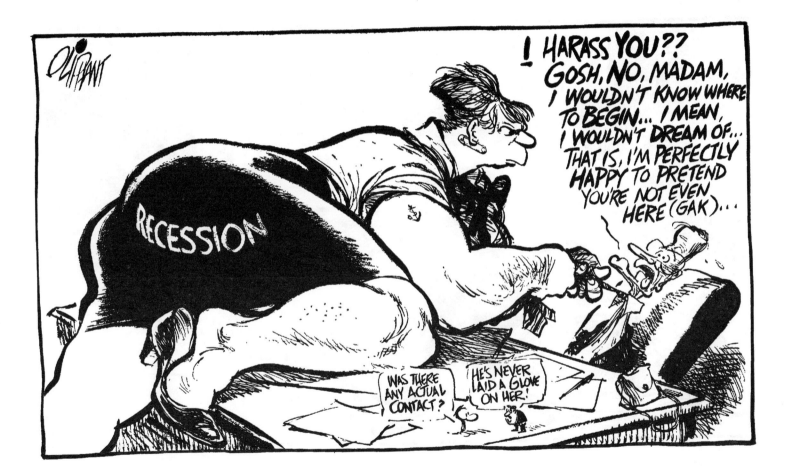

MAGIC HE AIN'T.

'ALL WE WANTED WAS A LITTLE ALIENATION.'

November 15, 1991

49

'WHAT RECESSION?' HE SAID.

'MAY I BE OF ASSISTANCE?'

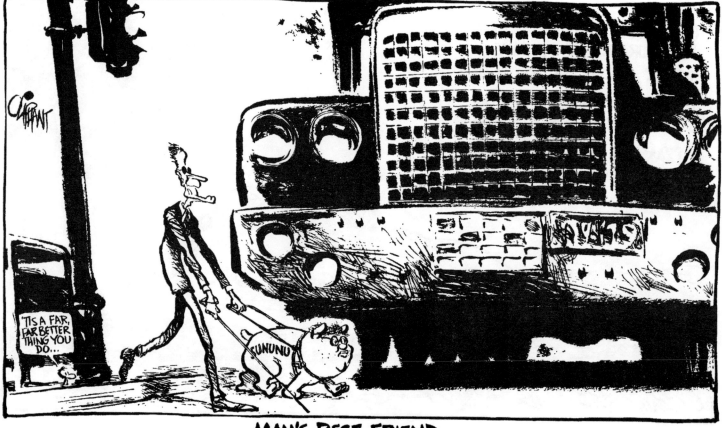

MAN'S BEST FRIEND.

December 5, 1991

55

'THE TRIAL OF WILLIAM KENNEDY SMITH WILL CONTINUE AFTER THESE MESSAGES...'

December 16, 1991

'WE, THE PEOPLE...'

'A THREE HUNDRED DOLLAR TAX REBATE — WHY, NOW WE CAN GET A NEW SOFA FOR THE DEN!'

'...FIRED MERRY CHRISTMAS, YOU'RE FIRED MERRY CHRISTMAS, YOU'RE FIRED...'

December 23, 1991

December 27, 1991

January 1, 1992

WHY WE ARE WHERE WE ARE.

January 13, 1992

GEORGE BUSH, IN FREE FALL, PAUSES TO ASK DIRECTIONS TO THE STATE OF THE UNION.

'OK, WE'RE READY TO FOLLOW YOU DOWN TO THE RIVER TO DROWN, BUT WE DON'T HEAR NO MUSIC!'

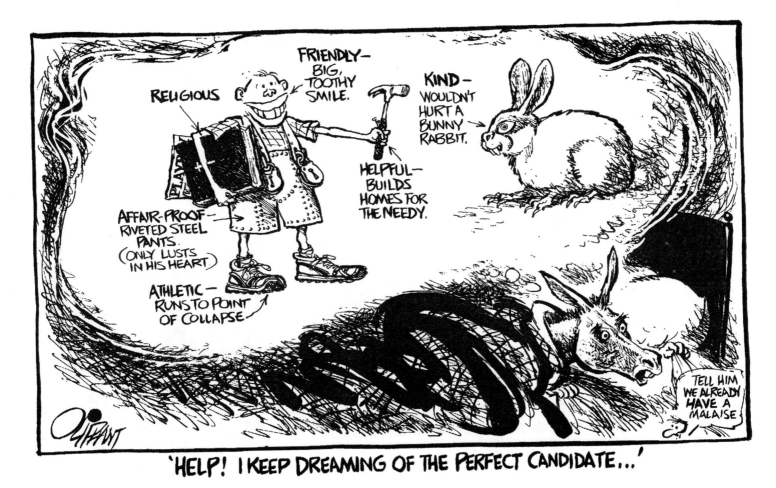

CURRENT STUDIES INDICATE SCHOOLS NEGLECT GIRLS IN FAVOR OF BOYS, WITH POSSIBLY DAMAGING RESULTS.

February 20, 1992

February 26, 1992

THEIR DOMESTIC ECONOMY A SHAMBLES, WORKERS STREAM ACROSS THE RIO GRANDE IN SEARCH OF WORK...

89

1992 CANDIDATES PRACTICAL EXAMS: THE PRE-BREAKFAST CHARACTER TEST.

'I BROKE MY PLEDGE ABOUT TAXES...'

THE 1992 BAD HOUSEKEEPING AWARD.

March 18, 1992

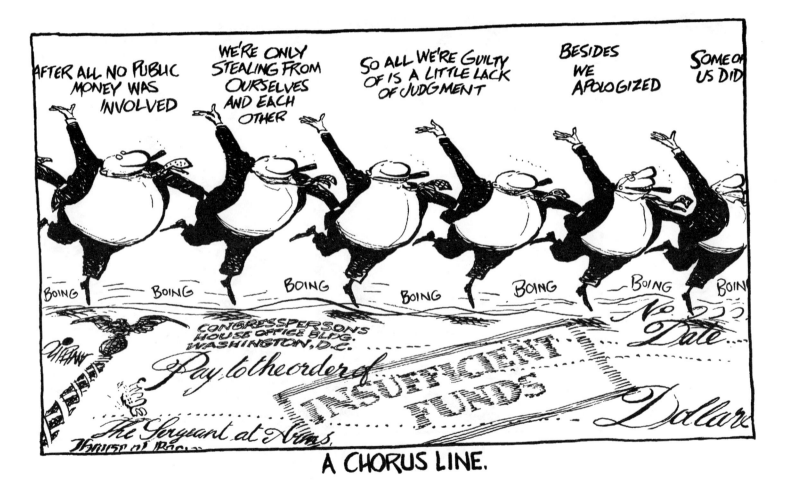

A CHORUS LINE.

99

THE DEMOCRATIC FIELD AT THIS TIME.

'THE GOOD NEWS IS YOUR SENTENCE HAS BEEN COMMUTED TO ONLY FOUR YEARS. THE BAD NEWS IS LEONA HELMSLEY MOVES IN WITH YOU APRIL 15!'

March 25, 1992

'I'M SORRY, MR. RUSHDIE, BUT MR. BUSH ISN'T IN RIGHT NOW... AND WOULD YOU PLEASE NOT STAND SO CLOSE WITH THAT NASTY THING.'

THE DEMOCRATIC FIELD — A STATUS REPORT.

WHILE THE OWNERS WERE ABSENT, THE SERVANTS OF THE PEOPLE HAD A WILD OLD PARTY UPSTAIRS.

April 8, 1992

'BUT THIS COULD SERIOUSLY HAMPER OUR ABILITY TO RUN AMOK!'

May 7, 1992

May 13, 1992

May 18, 1992

BUT, WAIT! WE NEED THIS MONEY FOR NATIONAL SECURITY - THE COMMIE MENACE COULD RETURN! AND WE HAVE TO HEAD OFF A SERBIAN INVASION! AND WHO WILL PROTECT OUR VITAL EXXON?... OR WE MAY HAVE TO NUKE THE NEA, OR SOMETHING...
..AND WE NEED IT FOR NATIONAL SECURITY!
CITIES

FOR OUR NEXT ACT...

May 20, 1992

...AND SO THE LOGGERS HAD JOBS AND WERE HAPPY, AND THE WISE OLD SPOTTED OWL WAS HAPPY, AND THEY ALL LIVED HAPPILY EVER AFTER.

May 22, 1992

May 27, 1992

1992: THE HAITIANS DISCOVER AMERICA.

May 28, 1992

123

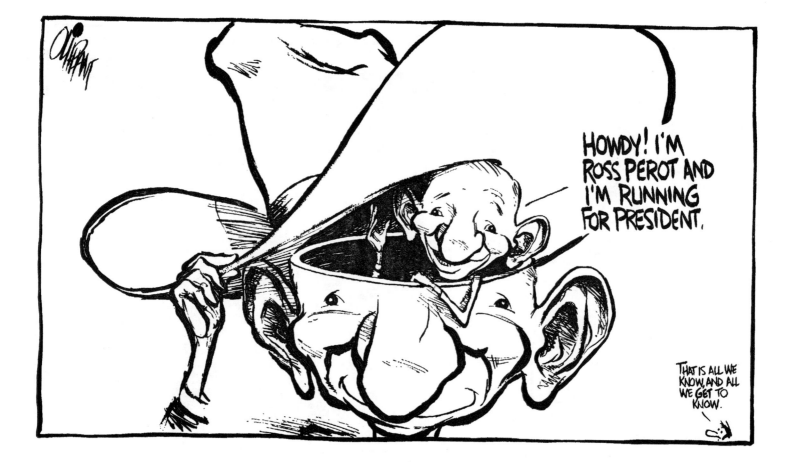

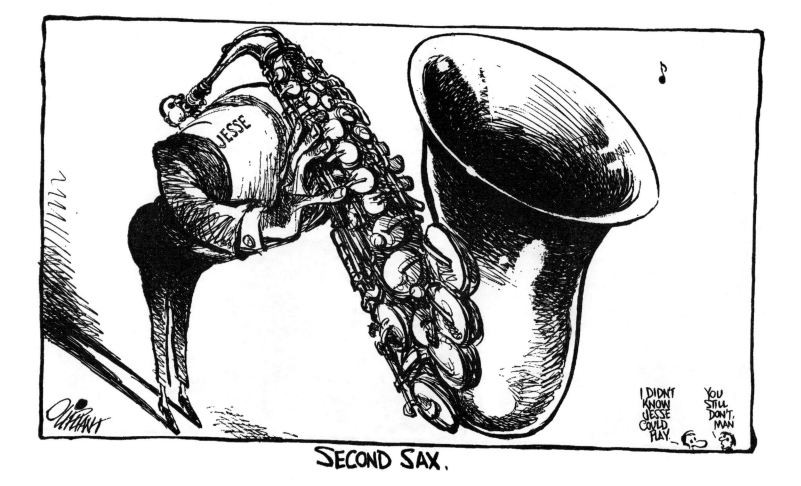

SECOND SAX.

MEANWHILE, AT A REMOTE ARMY BOOT-CAMP IN A LONELY PART OF THE BRITISH ISLES...

..THEN, RIGHT IN THE MIDDLE OF SUPPER, SOMEONE HAD TO ASK ABOUT A COHESIVE PROGRAM.

July 1, 1992

'PHEW! I'M GLAD I GOT THAT CAGE CLEANED OUT WITHOUT INCIDENT— NOW, WHERE DID I PUT THOSE DARN KEYS..?'

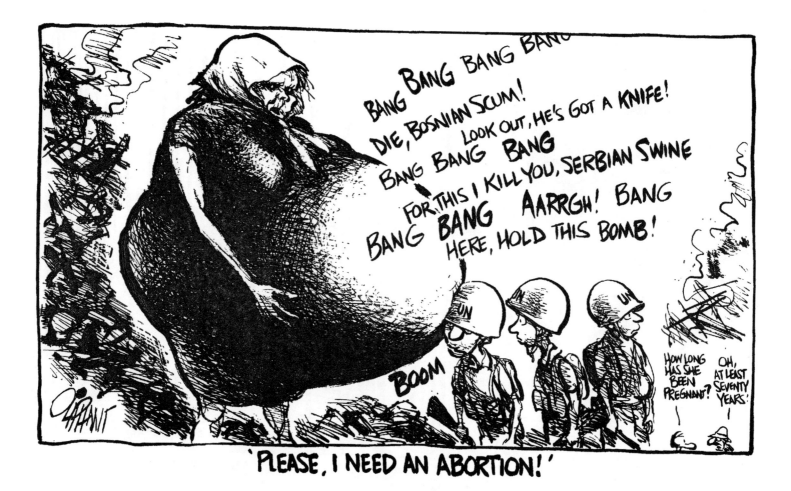

'PLEASE, I NEED AN ABORTION!'

'AH, THERE WE ARE, SIR. ALONG WITH STRONG FAMILY VALUES, OUR GOVERNMENT IS ALSO STRESSING FIVE SERVINGS OF FRUIT OR VEGETABLES PER DAY. BON APPETIT.'

July 16, 1992

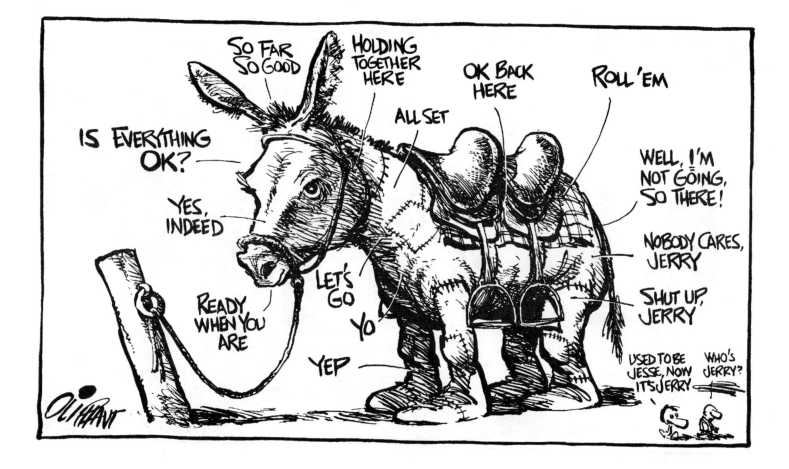

July 24, 1992

'ANY WORD YET IF I'M STILL ON THE TICKET?'

August 6, 1992

'PARDON ME — WHICH WAY TO THE QUAGMIRE?'

'AND WHAT KIND OF HEALTH INSURANCE DO YOU HAVE?'

August 10, 1992

154

'OH, IT'S THE BRAIN SURGEON—THANK GOD YOU'VE ARRIVED, DOCTOR! HURRY!'

August 17, 1992

'CALL THE AMERICANS AND ASK WHAT THEY INTEND DOING ABOUT ALL THIS!'

THE ETERNAL QUEST FOR SURVIVAL.

FAMILY.